CHEYENNE SWENSON

Dragons and their Colors

An Inspired Guide for Beginners to Realistically Color and Design Dragon Art

This book was professionally typeset on Reedsy.
Find out more at reedsy.com

Contents

Preface

Gaze into the sky, imagine it streaked with the vibrant hues of dragons in flight. These magnificent creatures, adorned in a spectrum of colors that shimmer with each beat of their vast wings, captivate the mind and stir the soul. The allure of these mythical beings, with scales that catch the light of the sun and eyes gleaming with ancient wisdom, has long inspired tales of wonder and awe. Yet, how often have we paused to consider not just their power and grace but the very colors they bear—colors that could tell stories of their lives, environments, and survival? The characteristics they possess—visually telling us that they lived in the mountain peaks or the marshes.

I am an artist, much like you, drawn irresistibly to the fusion of the fantastical and the real, particularly in the realm of dragons. My journey began in the humble corners of amateur sketching, where the first rough lines of these mythical creatures took flight on my canvas and in my mind. As my skills and understanding deepened, so did my fascination with bringing an element of realism to these beings of fantasy.

Dragons and their Colors: An Inspired Guide for Beginners to Realistically Color and Design Dragons is designed as a resource for you, to show you the ropes on how you can use just a little bit of research and enthusiasm to create a dragon. Whether you are seeking fresh vistas of inspiration or a complete newbie! Here, realism isn't just a style; it's a bridge connecting the fantastical with the plausible, making the mythical relatable through the study of real-world wildlife—the reptiles and birds whose colors are not merely for display but serve crucial roles in their survival, unless they are just for display.

This guide embarks on a structured exploration, beginning with foundational color theories. It then ventures into more advanced techniques, illustrating how to apply these principles specifically to dragon artwork. You'll learn to integrate your creations into believable environments and polish your pieces. Each chapter builds on the previous, ensuring a smooth progression that enhances your understanding.

As we journey through this book together, I invite you to push the boundaries of your creativity. Let the knowledge of nature's palette inspire you to experiment and innovate in your depictions of dragons. Imagine the possibilities when the camouflage of a chameleon or the iridescence of a hummingbird wing influences your dragon's design.

I still vividly remember my first encounter with the explosion of color and long lost beings. I was a little girl, no older than a kindergartner. My parents had taken me and my brother to the La Brea Tar Pits in Los Angeles. Having lived near the LA area for my more primitive years, it really wasn't that far of a drive from the suburbs of Simi Valley, merely an hour. But the world I was introduced to felt much further away. The white, brown, and tan skeletons of gigantic fauna that no longer roam America, the cold that blasts you as you step inside such a controlled environment, the black stinky tar that emanates throughout the air when you step outside the inside museum, and my most favorite memory, the magazine we got as a souvenir. The paleo art was astounding. It gave me an idea of what these creatures looked like, how they could have acted to one another in the cycle of predator and prey and especially survival. Sketches wouldn't have done justice, it was the color that brought them to life—the furs, the eyes, the fangs, the blood, the tar—the life of these long gone entities.

How did I get hooked on dragons then, you might be asking? Why the classic and renowned *How to train Your Dragon* of course! And my favorite dragon? Hookfang. For as much as the Nightfury held the spotlight as a main character, the fierceness of the beastly Monstrous Nightmare was much more intriguing.

And its color? Scales that of a red x burnt sienna and stripes to boot! When the dragon came out of it's cage in an explosion of fire, quickly scaling the chain dome as the colors were revealed as the flames extinguished? Even cooler. The tones of warm against cool drew me in.

This book, then, is more than just a manual; it is an invitation to explore, to dream, and to create. Let the colors of life inspire the dragons and other creatures that you bring to life on your canvas, making them as vivid in your artworks as they are in your imaginations. Together, let us recolor the skies with those of dragons, making the mythical visible in the light of our shared reality. These are my insights on how I think color can be used for fantastical realism, through some of my understanding and some research.

1

Dragons Across Cultures

Dragons, mythical creatures of immense power and symbolism, have permeated cultures across the globe for centuries. In this chapter, we will explore the rich tapestry of dragon lore, from the majestic and revered dragons of the East to the fearsome and treacherous dragons of the West, and even uncover some lesser-known dragons from around the world.

Eastern Dragons

Eastern dragons, particularly in Chinese and Japanese mythology, stand as symbols of wisdom, strength, and good fortune. Unlike their Western counterparts, Eastern dragons are often depicted as benevolent beings associated with natural elements like water and rain.

In Chinese mythology, dragons are revered as divine creatures capable of controlling the weather and bringing rain for a bountiful harvest. They are depicted as long, serpentine creatures with scaled bodies, often adorned with colorful patterns and majestic horns. The Chinese dragon is a potent symbol of imperial power and has been associated with the emperor since ancient times.

Japanese dragons, known as "ryū" or "tatsu," share many similarities with

Chinese dragons but possess their own distinct characteristics. Japanese folklore often portrays dragons as guardians of the sea or as protectors of sacred places. Unlike the more serpentine Chinese dragons, Japanese dragons are depicted with more reptilian features, including claws and wings. They are revered as powerful beings capable of both great destruction and profound wisdom.

Western Dragons

In Western mythology, dragons are often portrayed as malevolent creatures, hoarding treasure and terrorizing villages. These dragons are typically depicted as large, winged reptiles with scales, claws, and the ability to breathe fire. Western dragons embody themes of heroism, bravery, and the triumph of good over evil.

One of the most famous examples of a Western dragon is the dragon slain by Saint George in Christian legend. This dragon threatened a city until Saint George bravely slew it, symbolizing the triumph of Christianity over paganism. Similarly, in Norse mythology, the dragon Fafnir guards a hoard of treasure until he is defeated by the hero Sigurd.

Lesser Known Types of Dragons

Beyond the well-known dragons of Eastern and Western mythology, numerous cultures around the world have their own interpretations of these mythical creatures.

In Aztec mythology, Quetzalcoatl, the feathered serpent, was a prominent deity associated with creation and fertility. Quetzalcoatl was often depicted as a winged serpent with vibrant feathers, symbolizing the duality of life and death.

In Slavic folklore, the Zmey Gorynych is a three-headed dragon that terrorizes villages and captures princesses. Heroes like Dobrynya Nikitich and Ivan

Tsarevich are tasked with defeating this fearsome beast to save their kingdom.

Amphipteres

Amphipteres are fascinating creatures that originate from European heraldry and medieval bestiaries. These dragons are unique in that they possess wings but lack legs, giving them a serpentine appearance. Often depicted as serpents with feathered wings, amphipteres hold a distinct place in dragon lore due to their unusual anatomy. Despite their lack of legs, they are capable of flight, and their serpent-like bodies contribute to their mystique and allure. Amphipteres add a touch of intrigue to the rich tapestry of dragon mythology with their distinctive form and abilities.

Drakes

Drakes are a type of dragon that shares many similarities with their more renowned cousins but often differ in specific characteristics. Generally, drakes lack wings, distinguishing them from traditional dragons. However, they possess many other dragon-like features, including scales, reptilian appearance, and sometimes the ability to breathe fire. In various mythologies and fictional works, drakes often serve as formidable adversaries or powerful allies, embodying the awe-inspiring and mystical qualities associated with dragons while offering a unique twist with their wingless form.

Wyverns

Wyverns are legendary creatures that bear a striking resemblance to dragons but are distinct in several key aspects. Unlike traditional dragons, wyverns typically possess only two legs instead of four, along with a pair of wings and a long, serpentine tail. This unique anatomy gives them a more reptilian appearance and sets them apart from other dragon varieties. In various mythologies and folklore, wyverns are often depicted as fierce and formidable creatures, capable of flight and possessing potent abilities such as breathing fire or venomous attacks. Despite their differences from traditional dragons, wyverns remain iconic figures in fantasy literature, art, and popular culture, embodying the awe-inspiring and mythical qualities associated with these legendary beasts.

Hydras

The Hydra is a legendary creature from Greek mythology, often depicted as a multi-headed serpent or dragon. Its most famous portrayal comes from the myth of Heracles (Hercules) as one of his twelve laborers involved in slaying the Hydra. According to legend, when one of its heads was cut off, two more would grow in its place, making it a nearly invincible foe. The Hydra symbolizes the challenges in life that seem insurmountable, requiring great strength and perseverance to overcome.

In conclusion, dragons have left an indelible mark on cultures worldwide, embodying a wide range of meanings and interpretations. From the revered dragons of the East to the feared dragons of the West and the lesser-known dragons of various cultures, these mythical creatures continue to captivate the human imagination, inspiring tales of heroism, adventure, and the eternal struggle between good and evil.

2

Foundation of Color Theory

Color theory forms the backbone of artistic expression, providing artists with the knowledge to create visually compelling and emotionally resonant artwork. In this chapter, we explore the foundational principles of color theory and how they can be applied to depict dragons with depth, realism, and emotional impact.

Understanding the Color Wheel

The color wheel is a fundamental tool for understanding the relationships between colors and their various properties. It consists of primary colors (red, blue, and yellow), secondary colors (green, orange, and purple), and tertiary colors (mixtures of primary and secondary colors). By understanding the principles of color harmony, artists can create visually pleasing compositions that effectively communicate their artistic vision.

When depicting dragons, artists can use the color wheel to choose complementary or analogous color schemes that enhance the overall aesthetic appeal of their artwork. Complementary colors, situated opposite each other on the color wheel, create contrast and vibrancy, while analogous colors, located next to each other, produce a sense of harmony and cohesion.

Color Temperature Basics

Color temperature refers to the perceived warmth or coolness of a color and plays a significant role in setting the mood and atmosphere of an artwork. Warm colors (reds, oranges, and yellows) evoke feelings of warmth, energy, and intensity, while cool colors (blues, greens, and purples) convey a sense of calmness, serenity, and tranquility.

When coloring dragons, artists can use color temperature to convey various aspects of their personality and environment. A dragon associated with fire and heat may be depicted using warm, fiery hues, while a dragon dwelling in icy mountains or deep oceans may be portrayed using cool, frosty tones.

The color of fire—if your dragon happens to have fire—is influenced by the temperature of the burning material and the presence of specific chemical elements. Fire changes color as it gets hotter due to changes in the composition of the flames and the emission of light.

- **Chemical Composition**: Different materials burn with different flame colors due to the chemicals present in them. For example, a fire fueled by wood might have a yellow-orange flame due to the presence of carbon, while a fire fueled by alcohol might have a blue flame due to the presence of carbon and hydrogen.
- **Temperature and Energy Levels**: As the temperature of the fire increases, more energy is available for the excitation of atoms and molecules in the flames. This leads to the emission of light at shorter wavelengths, which corresponds to colors towards the blue end of the spectrum. Cooler fires emit light at longer wavelengths, which corresponds to colors towards the red end of the spectrum.
- **Blackbody Radiation**: Fire emits light through a process called blackbody radiation. As the temperature increases, the peak wavelength of this radiation shifts towards shorter wavelengths, leading to changes in color perception. Cooler fires emit predominantly red and orange light, while hotter fires emit blue and white light. Ever ignite your stove top?

- **Presence of Chemicals**: Certain chemicals, when present in the flames, can produce distinctive colors. For example, the presence of copper can give flames a green color, while the presence of sodium can produce a yellow flame. These colors become more prominent as the temperature of the fire increases and the atoms or molecules of these chemicals are excited to higher energy levels.

Enough of some niche interest in fire for element relations, let's talk about how color actually affects say reptiles...

Reptiles can be influenced by their temperature, particularly in species that are ectothermic, meaning their body temperature is regulated by external sources such as sunlight.

- **Behavioral Thermoregulation**: Reptiles often engage in behavior known as thermoregulation, where they seek out specific temperature zones in their environment to maintain their body temperature within a certain range. Different temperatures can affect the expression of pigments in their skin or scales.
- **Melanin Production**: Temperature can influence the production and distribution of melanin, the pigment responsible for dark colors. In cooler temperatures, reptiles may produce more melanin, resulting in darker skin or scales. Conversely, in warmer temperatures, melanin production may decrease, leading to lighter coloration.
- **Physiological Changes**: Changes in temperature can also affect other physiological processes that influence coloration, such as blood flow and hydration levels. For example, when a reptile basks in the sun to warm up, blood vessels near the skin dilate, causing the skin to appear redder. On the flip side, when it's colder and the reptile hides away, the skin can appear duller.
- **Adaptations to Environment**: The extent to which temperature influences coloration can vary depending on the species and its natural habitat.

Reptiles living in environments with significant temperature fluctuations may exhibit more pronounced color changes compared to species in more stable climates.

Overall, while temperature can influence the coloration of reptiles, it's just one of many factors that contribute to their appearance. Other factors include genetics, diet, age, and environmental conditions.

Why do I bring these very specific examples up? It's to give you an idea of how to think of the realistic factors. Art is like a story, just very visual, sometimes with words, but mostly without. If someone were to ask you, 'Why does your dragon have green fire?' or ' Why is it blue if it's in the forest?' Would you have a story to give them? Could you explain yourself as to why these elements were added? I encourage you to take backstory into account, your art will thank you later. A little research goes a long way.

Color and Emotion: Setting the Mood with Hues

Color has the power to evoke strong emotions and associations, making it a powerful tool for setting the mood and tone of an artwork. Different colors are often associated with specific emotions and themes, allowing artists to convey complex narratives and atmospheres through their choice of hues.

For example, red is often associated with passion, energy, and danger, while blue evokes feelings of calmness, serenity, and introspection. Artists can use these associations to imbue their depiction of dragons with emotional depth and resonance, enhancing the viewer's connection to the artwork. Furthermore, colors carry cultural and symbolic significance that can vary widely across different societies and historical periods. For instance, red may symbolize love and vitality in one culture but signify danger or warning in another. By understanding the cultural context and symbolic meanings of colors, artists can imbue their artwork with layers of depth and meaning, enriching the viewer's interpretation and engagement with the piece.

Thematic Coloring

Or in simpler terms, a color palette. Choosing how you wish to present your piece comes with a lot of challenges, especially choosing said colors. Creating depth and dimension in dragon artwork often involves layering colors to build up richness and complexity. By carefully applying multiple layers of color, artists can achieve a sense of texture and depth in the dragon's scales, skin, and other features. This technique allows for subtle variations in hue and tone, enhancing the overall realism and impact of the artwork.

When layering colors for dragons, artists may choose to start with a base color that serves as the foundation for the dragon's overall color scheme. Additional layers of lighter and darker shades can then be applied to create highlights and shadows, adding depth and dimension to the dragon's form. For digital, play with opacities and layers. For traditional, sheer paints and other tools that give a sheer color can build upon each other, possibly giving you an outcome you never would have thought of.

Granted, not everyone likes a ton of color on the page, and monochromatic palettes work just as well. What is monochromatism you may ask? Monochromatic means containing or using only one color, but in the form of a palette, it would appear as a gradient, from the light version of the color to its darker version. For easily accessible palettes that are online I suggest *coolors.co*. You can create any amount of combinations you could possibly imagine, even already made ones to make it easier.

Select the colors you want to use in your artwork. Consider how they blend together and create harmony or contrast. It's helpful to have a basic understanding of color theory, such as complementary, analogous, or triadic color schemes.

- **Base Layer**: Begin with a base layer of color on your canvas or paper. This layer sets the foundation for your artwork and provides a background for further layers. Choose a color that represents the overall tone or mood you want to achieve.

- **Dark to Light**: Work from dark to light (or vice versa). There are different approaches to layering colors, but a common one is to start with darker colors and gradually build up to lighter ones, or vice versa. This helps in achieving depth and dimension in your artwork.

- **Layers**: Use translucent or transparent colors for layering. If you're working with traditional mediums like paint, allow each layer to dry completely before adding the next layer. This prevents colors from blending together unintentionally and gives you more control and allows the colors underneath to show through, creating a rich and luminous effect. Watercolor and acrylic glazing techniques are good examples of this approach. Layering colors is a skill that improves with practice. Don't be afraid to experiment with different colors, techniques, and layering orders to see what works best for your artwork. Over time, you'll develop your own style and preferences.

As you add more layers, step back occasionally to assess your artwork. You can make adjustments or refinements as needed to achieve the desired effect. This might involve adding more layers to intensify colors, blending edges, or adding highlights and shadows.

Layering colors can be time-consuming, especially if you're working with multiple layers or waiting for paint to dry between layers. Practice patience and enjoy the process of gradually building up your artwork.

Remember, there's no right or wrong way to layer colors, so don't be afraid to experiment and have fun with it!

3

Mastering Environmental Integration

Evaluating environmental integration in dragon art is crucial as it enhances the realism and impact of the depiction, allowing viewers to suspend disbelief and fully immerse themselves in the fantastical world portrayed. This involves considering factors such as lighting, perspective, and landscape features to create a believable and immersive scene.

The Role of Environment in Dragon Coloration

The environment plays a crucial role in shaping the coloration of dragons and other animals, as they often adapt to blend in with their surroundings or reflect the elements they are associated with. Dragons dwelling in lush forests may exhibit earthy tones and vibrant greens, while dragons inhabiting volcanic regions may display cool toned reds, blacks, and browns.

Say a green heron is perched in a tree. The bright green of the leaves leave it standing out like a sore thumb. This is not its habitat for foraging. Green herons search for prey in more aquatic habitats such as marshes, mangroves, creeks, swamps and streams. The greenish-gray plumage helps it blend into its surroundings while hunting for fish and small amphibians.

Dragons are intrinsically linked to their environment. Habitat consideration is essential when depicting dragons, as their environments shape their appearance, behavior, and interactions with the world around them. Dragons may inhabit diverse landscapes ranging from lush forests and misty mountains to desolate deserts and deep oceans, each with its own unique features and challenges.

When creating dragon artwork, artists must carefully consider the habitat in which their subjects reside. A dragon dwelling in a forested region may be surrounded by towering trees, lush vegetation, and abundant wildlife, while a dragon living in a volcanic landscape may navigate treacherous terrain filled with molten lava and billowing smoke.

By accurately depicting the habitat of their subjects, artists can create a sense of realism and immersion that draws viewers into the fantastical worlds inhabited by dragons, enriching the narrative and visual impact of their artwork.

Utilizing Flora and Fauna

Flora and fauna play an integral role in shaping the ecosystems inhabited by dragons, providing food, shelter, and resources essential for survival. When creating dragon artwork, artists can utilize flora and fauna to enhance the sense of realism and environmental immersion in their compositions.

For example, a dragon depicted in a forested habitat may be surrounded by lush vegetation, towering trees, and diverse wildlife, such as birds, deer, and small mammals. By incorporating these elements into their artwork, artists can create a dynamic and vibrant scene that reflects the diversity and complexity of the natural world.

Likewise, dragons may interact with flora and fauna in various ways, such as hunting for prey, seeking shelter in dense foliage, or utilizing natural resources for camouflage or defense. By depicting these interactions, artists can further enrich the narrative and character development of their subjects, adding depth and complexity to their artwork.

Furthermore, dragons could adapt characteristics to better survive in said environment.

Let's take the leopard gecko for example, they're one of my favorite little guys. Leopard geckos have adapted to thrive in their natural environment through several key features:

1. **Nocturnal Lifestyle**: Leopard geckos are primarily nocturnal, meaning they are most active during the night. This adaptation allows them to avoid the extreme heat of the day in their native habitat, which is typically the rocky deserts and arid regions of Afghanistan, Pakistan, and parts of India.

2. **Camouflage and Coloration**: Their natural coloration and patterns provide excellent camouflage against their rocky desert habitat, helping them blend into their surroundings and avoid predators. Their mottled skin, with various shades of yellow, cream, brown, and sometimes orange or pink, allows them to blend in seamlessly with the desert rocks.

3. **Heat Tolerance**: Leopard geckos have evolved to tolerate high temperatures during the day and lower temperatures at night. They have specialized heat-sensing organs on their heads, known as loreal pits, which help them detect prey and navigate their environment by sensing infrared radiation.

4. **Water Conservation**: In their arid habitat, water is scarce, so leopard geckos have developed adaptations to conserve moisture. They have efficient kidneys that produce concentrated urine, minimizing water loss. Additionally, they can obtain water from their food, such as insects and small vertebrates.

5. **Burrowing Behavior**: Leopard geckos are skilled burrowers, using their strong claws to dig burrows in sandy or loose soil. This behavior allows them to escape the heat of the day and seek refuge from predators, as well as providing a cooler, more stable microclimate for resting and hiding.

6. **Communication and Fat Storage**: In some cases, the tail may also be used in communication between leopard geckos. Tail waving or vibrating may serve as a form of communication, signaling aggression, submission,

or territorial boundaries to other geckos. Leopard geckos also store fat reserves in their tails, which they can draw upon during periods of scarcity or stress. This adaptation allows them to survive in their arid desert habitats, where food sources may be intermittent.

Overall, leopard geckos have evolved a suite of adaptations that enable them to thrive in the harsh desert environments where they are found. These adaptations help them regulate body temperature, conserve water, avoid predators, and locate prey, making them well-suited to their natural habitat. Would your dragon have to forage everyday? Or would it have other characteristics that enable it to thrive?

Water and Terrain Influences

Water and terrain influences are significant factors to consider when integrating environments into dragon artwork. Dragons may inhabit diverse landscapes, from rugged mountains and expansive plains to deep oceans and winding rivers, each presenting unique challenges and opportunities for artistic expression.

When depicting dragons in aquatic environments, artists can incorporate elements such as underwater caves, coral reefs, and marine life to create immersive and visually stunning compositions. Dragons may interact with water in various ways, such as diving for fish, basking in the sun on rocky outcrops, or engaging in aerial battles above the waves.

Similarly, terrain influences such as mountains, valleys, and canyons can dramatically impact the appearance and behavior of dragons. Dragons dwelling in mountainous regions may have adaptations such as strong wings and muscular limbs for navigating steep slopes and rugged terrain, while dragons living in open plains may rely on speed and agility to hunt prey and evade predators.

By carefully considering water and terrain influences, artists can create dynamic and engaging compositions that showcase the diversity and beauty of the natural world while highlighting the majestic presence of dragons within it.

Take for example the marine iguana, one of four other iguana to inhabit the Galápagos Islands. It's the only marine lizard in the world. Marine iguana have evolved several unique adaptations to thrive in their harsh marine environment in the Galápagos Islands:

1. **Salt Excretion**: Marine iguanas feed primarily on marine algae, which are high in salt content. To cope with the excess salt intake, marine iguanas have specialized salt glands located near their nasal passages. These glands allow them to expel excess salt from their bodies through nasal excretion, preventing dehydration and maintaining electrolyte balance.
2. **Efficient Swimming**: Unlike other iguana species, marine iguanas are highly adapted for swimming. They have flattened tails for propulsion and powerful limbs with long claws, which they use to grip rocks and navigate underwater currents while foraging for algae.
3. **Thermal Regulation**: The marine environment can be cold, and marine iguanas must regulate their body temperature to avoid hypothermia. They bask in the sun on rocky shores to absorb heat, then dive into the cool ocean waters to feed. This behavior allows them to maintain optimal body temperature while minimizing energy expenditure.
4. **Reduced Metabolic Rate**: To conserve energy during long periods of underwater foraging, marine iguanas have a lower metabolic rate compared to terrestrial iguanas. They can slow down their heart rate and oxygen consumption while diving, allowing them to stay submerged for extended periods without needing to resurface for air.
5. **Cryptic Coloration**: Marine iguanas often have dark coloration, which helps them absorb heat from the sun more efficiently. Additionally, their coloration provides camouflage against the dark volcanic rocks of their coastal habitats, making them less visible to predators such as birds of prey.
6. **Large Size**: Marine iguanas are one of the largest species of iguanas, with adult males reaching lengths of up to 1.5 meters (5 feet). Their large size may provide advantages in thermoregulation, predator avoidance, and

competition for resources in their coastal habitats.

These unique adaptations allow marine iguanas to exploit a niche in the Galápagos Islands that is inaccessible to most other reptiles, making them a fascinating example of evolutionary specialization in response to environmental challenges.

Seasonal and Time-Afflicted Influences and Variations

Environmental factors such as the changing seasons and the passage of time can also influence the appearance of dragons in artwork. For example, dragons depicted in winter may be portrayed with icy blue scales and frost-covered wings, while dragons depicted in autumn may be adorned with fiery reds and golden yellows.

Similarly, dragons depicted during different times of day may be bathed in the warm glow of the sun or shrouded in the cool shadows of twilight. By considering these seasonal and time-afflicted influences, artists can create artwork that is rich in detail and evocative of the natural world.

Moisture and dryness effects are crucial considerations when depicting dragons, as these environmental factors can significantly influence the appearance of their scales and overall coloration. Dragons dwelling in humid environments, such as tropical rainforests or misty mountains, may exhibit characteristics that reflect their surroundings. Their scales might appear glossy and iridescent, reflecting light like polished gemstones. Artists can achieve this effect by using techniques like glazing or applying a gloss medium to certain areas of the dragon's body.

Additionally, moisture-laden air can enhance the vibrancy of colors, making them appear more saturated and vivid. Artists may choose to incorporate rich, lush hues into their depiction of dragons in humid environments, emphasizing the abundance of life and vitality in their surroundings.

Dragons inhabiting dry or arid regions, such as deserts or barren wastelands, may display characteristics indicative of their harsh environment. Their scales may appear matte and weathered, with subtle textures and variations in coloration that evoke the parched earth and sun-bleached landscapes.

To simulate dryness effects, artists can employ techniques like dry brushing or stippling to create a rough, textured surface on the dragon's scales. By using earthy tones and muted colors, they can convey the arid nature of the dragon's habitat, with hues reminiscent of sand, dust, and weathered rock formations.

Now dragons may not have scales whatsoever! I've mentioned scales strictly because this is a beginners guide, but if you were to mess around with the idea of your dragon having skin rather than scales that's something entirely different. But I'd like to bing up something I find rather intriguing that could help you understand what I'm trying to explain: hair color.

Do you ever go out and see yourself in a reflection of sorts and see how your hair has "changed" color? This is thanks to lighting and possibly other environmental factors, but I'll focus on the lighting.

1. **Warm, Incandescent Lighting**: Warm incandescent lighting emits a soft, yellowish glow that can enhance the appearance of hair, making it appear brighter and warmer. The warm tones of incandescent light complement the natural hues of hair, particularly shades of blonde, red, and brown, by accentuating their warmth and depth. Incandescent lighting tends to have a color temperature in the range of 2700K to 3000K, which falls on the warmer end of the spectrum. This warm light can create a flattering ambiance, especially in indoor settings like homes, restaurants, or theaters, where it adds a cozy and inviting atmosphere. When hair is illuminated by warm incandescent lighting, it can produce a soft, golden glow that enhances its natural highlights and lowlights. This effect is often desirable in photography, cinematography, and interior design, where the warm, flattering light can create a sense of warmth

and intimacy.

2. **Warm, Yellowish Light**: The warm undertones present in hair, particularly in shades of blonde, red, and brown can make hair appear richer and more vibrant, enhancing its natural warmth and depth. However, in some cases, excessively warm lighting can also intensify yellow tones in hair, especially if the lighting has a strong yellow cast. This effect may be more noticeable in lighter hair colors, where the yellowish hue becomes more prominent. The perceived color of hair under different lighting conditions can also depend on the overall color balance of the lighting environment. For example, warmer light settings may create a more cohesive color palette when combined with warm-colored walls or décor, but they may also affect the accuracy of color representation

3. **Warmer, Orange-based Light**: Orange-based lighting, such as warm incandescent or tungsten lights, can accentuate the warm tones present in hair. This can lead to hair appearing richer and more vibrant, with golden or honey undertones becoming more pronounced. In some cases, particularly for hair that already has underlying warm tones or has been dyed blonde or light brown, orange-based lighting can intensify any brassiness present in the hair. Brassiness refers to unwanted warm, yellow, or orange tones that can develop in hair, especially after bleaching or color treatments. The overall color balance and composition of the lighting environment can also influence how hair color is perceived. Warm orange lighting may create a cohesive color palette when combined with warm-colored walls or décor, but it may also exaggerate any warm or brassy tones in hair.

4. **Cold White or Bluish Light**: Cold white or bluish lights can indeed have an impact on the appearance of hair color, potentially making it appear more ash-blonde in tone. Cold white or bluish lights have a higher color temperature, typically in the range of 4000K to 6500K, which creates a cooler, more neutral lighting environment. In contrast to warm lighting, which accentuates warm tones in hair, cooler lighting can help neutralize or minimize warm or golden undertones, making hair appear cooler in color. Ash-blonde hair is characterized by cool, muted tones with

hints of gray or blue. Cold white or bluish lights can enhance these ashy tones, giving the hair a cooler, more subdued appearance. This effect is particularly noticeable in blonde hair colors, where the cool lighting can intensify the ashiness and reduce any warmth or brassiness. Cooler lighting environments can provide more accurate color representation, particularly for hair colors with cool undertones. This can be beneficial for assessing the true color of ash-blonde hair and ensuring that it appears as intended, without being influenced by warm or yellow lighting.

5. **Fluorescent or LED Lights**: Fluorescent and LED lights often have a cooler color temperature compared to incandescent or warm white lights. While fluorescent lights can vary in color temperature, many emit a bluish-white or cool white light, while LED lights can range from cool white to daylight color temperatures. These cooler light sources can wash out warm tones in hair, making it appear cooler and less vibrant. Fluorescent and LED lights may not provide the same level of color rendering as incandescent lights, meaning they may not accurately represent the true colors of objects, including hair. This reduced color rendering can contribute to the perception of dullness in hair color under fluorescent or LED lighting. Cooler lighting environments created by fluorescent or LED lights can neutralize warm or golden undertones in hair, making it appear cooler in tone. This effect is particularly noticeable in blonde hair colors, where the cooler lighting can reduce warmth and minimize brassiness.

In conclusion, mastering environmental integration is essential for creating immersive and captivating dragon artwork. By considering habitat considerations, utilizing flora and fauna, and incorporating water and terrain influences, artists can bring their fantastical worlds to life, inviting viewers to explore the rich tapestry of environments inhabited by these mythical creatures.

4

Continuing Your Journey

Throughout our journey exploring how to color, we've delved into the intricate nuances that make these mythical creatures not only visually stunning but emotionally resonant. From the possible fiery reds of the ferocious wyverns to the plausible tranquil blues of the wise and ancient drakes, each hue carries with it its own narrative weight, shaping the very essence of the dragon it adorns.

But our exploration doesn't stop at mere color; it extends into the realms of environment and storytelling. Placing our dragons within meticulously crafted habitats, we've learned to harness the power of lighting, weather, and detailed landscapes to breathe life into our creations. By anchoring dragons within environments that reflect their characteristics, we elevate them from mere subjects of art to pivotal players in our narratives, capable of carrying thematic weight and emotional resonance.

Indeed, dragons are not just fantastic beasts—they're conduits through which we explore complex themes, evoke powerful emotions, and craft compelling stories. As artists, it's our duty to honor these creatures by continually honing our craft, delving deeper into their lore, and pushing the boundaries of our creativity.

I urge you to continue your learning journey, to seek out both online and offline art communities for feedback, inspiration, and support. Engage with fellow artists, share your knowledge, and never cease to explore the vast expanse of dragon artistry, intimidating as it may be for some of you, I know it is for me.

Thank you for joining me on this artistic odyssey. Your dedication and passion are truly inspiring. As you continue to explore and master the art of dragon crafting, remember that the sky's the limit. Keep creating, keep learning, and above all, keep dreaming.

5

Sources

Barnhart, B. (2023, December 5). *Color psychology in art and design.* Linearity Blog. https://www.linearity.io/blog/color-psychology/

Coolors - The super fast color palettes generator! (n.d.). Coolors.co. https://-coolors.co/

De Guzman, C. (2024, February 6). This Lunar New Year is the Year of the Dragon: Why the beast is a big deal in Chinese culture. *TIME.* https://time.co m/6691804/china-dragons-symbolism-history-significance-new-year/

Drawing Dragon Anatomy, Step by step, Drawing Guide, by Dawn - DragoArt. (n.d.). https://dragoart.com/tut/drawing-dragon-anatomy-20733

Education, J. G. M. (2022). 15 Unique examples of animal adaptations. In *YourDictionary.* https://www.yourdictionary.com/articles/animal-adaptation s-examples

Fantastical Biology – Part One: fantasy creatures and their habitats. (2014, May 28). http://fantasy-faction.com/2014/fantastical-biology-fantasy-creatures -and-their-habitats

Figaro. (2020, December 28). *What's my actual hair colour? (It seems to be different in every mirror ...).* Hair & Beauty Salon Near Old Street | Figaro London. https://www.figarolondon.uk/whats-my-actual-hair-colour-it-seems-to-b

e-different-in-every-mirror/#:~:text=In%20warmer%2C%20yellowish%2
0light%20settings,to%20be%20more%20ash%2Dblonde.

Gamblin Artist Colors. (2021, August 25). *Understanding Color Temperature within Painting - Gamblin Artists Colors*. Gamblin Artists Colors. https://gambli ncolors.com/understanding-color-temperature/

King, M. (2023, June 28). *The Eye of the Beholder: How lighting affects our color perception*. NIST. https://www.nist.gov/blogs/taking-measure/eye-beho lder-how-lighting-affects-our-color-perception

Kruzer, A. (2022, March 8). *How to build a favorable habitat for your leopard gecko*. The Spruce Pets. https://www.thesprucepets.com/leopard-gecko-habi tat-5199607#:~:text=Leopard%20geckos%20are%20native%20to,they%20 can%20enter%20semi%2Dhibernation.

Lowell Milken Center for Unsung Heroes. (2023). *Storytelling through Art* [Lesson Plan]. https://www.lowellmilkencenter.org/assets/lesson-plans/Sto rytelling-Through-Art/AE-Storytellling-Through-Art-Lesson-Plan-FINAL. pdf

McNee, L. (2010, September 29). *How to Paint Iridescent Bird Feathers & Make Them Glow*. Lori McNee - Fine Art & Tips. https://lorimcnee.com/how-to-pai nt-iridescent-bird-feathers-make-them-glow/

Oceana. (2023, May 18). *Marine Iguana | Oceana*. https://oceana.org/marine -life/marine-iguana/

OldWorldGods. (2023, November 28). Naga Myth: Unveiling the Serpentine Legends and Folklore from Asia - Old World Gods. *Old World Gods*. https://old worldgods.com/indian/naga-myth/

Scott, D. (2024, April 3). *A comprehensive guide to color theory for artists*. Draw Paint Academy. https://drawpaintacademy.com/a-comprehensive-guide-to-color-theory-for-artists/

Swinton, D. (2023, August 20). 7 Benefits of Painting with a Limited Palette. *Swinton's Art Supply*. https://www.swintonsart.com/post/7-benefits-of-paint ing-with-a-limited-palette

Team, D. (2023, July 31). *7 Tips for Better Color Theory in Realistic Painting*. Daisie Blog. https://blog.daisie.com/7-tips-for-better-color-theory-in-real istic-painting/#:~:text=Use%20warm%20colors%20for%20the,how%20it

%20makes%20you%20feel.

Valerie. (2024, February 28). *Animal Disguises: types of camouflage and coloration!* Wild Earth Lab. https://wildearthlab.com/2024/02/21/camouflage -and-aposematism/

Where Modern Dragon designs came from – Maegan A. Stebbins – Maverick-Werewolf's Den. (n.d.). https://maverickwerewolf.com/articles/where-moder n-dragon-designs-came-from/

Wikipedia contributors. (2024a, March 27). *Animal coloration.* Wikipedia. https://en.wikipedia.org/wiki/Animal_coloration#:~:text=Some%20animals %20are%20coloured%20for,to%20carry%20oxygen%20is%20red.

Wikipedia contributors. (2024b, March 27). *Animal coloration.* Wikipedia. https://en.wikipedia.org/wiki/Animal_coloration